The Twelve Days of Christmas

[Correspondence]

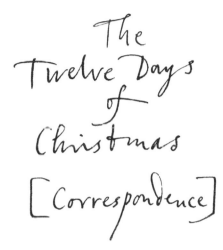

First published in Great Britain in 1998 by Doubleday,
a division of Transworld Publishers Ltd.

This edition published in Great Britain in 2013 by
Atlantic Books, an imprint of Atlantic Books Ltd.

10 9 8 7 6 5 4 3 2 1

A CIP catalogue record for this book is available from the British Library.

Hardback ISBN: 978 1 78239 223 1

[Printed by Novoprint S.A.]

Atlantic Books
An imprint of Atlantic Books Ltd
Ormond House
26–27 Boswell Street
London WC1N 3JZ
www.atlantic-books.co.uk

John Julius Norwich

The
TWELVE DAYS
of
CHRISTMAS
[Correspondence]

illustrated by
Quentin Blake

Atlantic Books
LONDON

Foreword

It all starts so well. I imagine that Edward is a hearty young fellow, richer than the dreams of the Rich List, who met Emily at a party arranged by a friend. He is taken by her ladylike qualities (carefully instilled by Mummy) and her quiet modesty. He proposes marriage and she blushingly accepts. Mummy is thrilled. Emily prepares herself for a yearning absence over Christmas, but he promises to send a little surprise to her and swears undying love. Red-faced with glee, he sets about some serious wooing.

Christmas presents are more thrilling when they are unexpected, and at first Edward hits the right note: a pretty (and tiny) tree, a little bird, a darling friend to chirrup his affection while the young lovers are apart... what could be more charming? Greatly encouraged by her first extravagant note of thanks, Edward launches into his extended plan. But he fails to heed the warning signs in her ensuing letters and what started as a fairy tale begins to skid off the rails and start across the field at full throttle, because what Edward True Love never knew is that with a girl like Emily, Less really is More.

As we sing the jolly and familiar Christmas song we would do well to remember Emily, and Mummy, and Edward's notion of generosity. I would draw your attention to the pictures towards the end of the book, a warning – if ever there was one – against extreme partying. Between them, John Julius Norwich and Quentin Blake have happily created a far more acceptable present: a perfect little book.

Joanna Lumley

25th December

My dearest darling – That partridge, in that
lovely little pear tree! What an enchanting,
romantic, poetic present! Bless you and thank you.

Your deeply loving Emily

26th December

My dearest darling Edward – The two turtle doves arrived this morning and are cooing away in the pear tree as I write. I'm so touched and grateful.

With undying love, as always, Emily.

27th December

My darling Edward – You do think of the most
original presents; whoever thought of sending
anybody three French hens? Do they really come
all the way from France? It's a pity that we have no
chicken coops, but I expect we'll find some.
Thank you, anyway, they're heaven.

Your loving Emily

28th December

*D*earest Edward – What a surprise – four
calling birds arrived this morning. They are very
sweet, even if they do call rather loudly – they
make telephoning impossible. But I expect they'll
calm down when they get used to their new home.
Anyway, I'm very grateful – of course I am.

Love from Emily

29th December

*D*earest Edward – The postman has just delivered
five most beautiful gold rings, one for each finger,
and all fitting perfectly. A really lovely present –
lovelier in a way than birds, which do take rather a
lot of looking after. The four that arrived yesterday
are still making a terrible row, and I'm afraid none of
us got much sleep last night. Mummy says she wants
to use the rings to 'wring' their necks – she's only
joking, I think; though I know what she means.
But I *love* the rings. Bless you.

Love, Emily

Dear Edward – Whatever I expected to find
when I opened the front door this morning,
it certainly wasn't six socking great geese laying
eggs all over the doorstep. Frankly, I rather hoped
you had stopped sending me birds – we have no
room for them and they have already ruined
the croquet lawn. I know you meant well, but –
let's call a halt, shall we?

Love, Emily

31st December

Edward – I thought I said no more birds; but this morning I woke up to find no less than seven swans all trying to get into our tiny goldfish pond. I'd rather not think what happened to the goldfish. The whole house seems to be full of birds – to say nothing of what they leave behind them. Please, please STOP.

Your Emily

Frankly, I think I prefer birds. What am I to do
with eight milkmaids – AND their cows? Is this
some kind of joke? If so, I'm afraid I don't find it
very amusing.

Emily

2nd January

Look here, Edward, this has gone far enough.
You say you're sending me nine ladies dancing;
all I can say is that judging from the way they dance,
they're certainly not ladies. The village just isn't
accustomed to seeing a regiment of shameless hussies
with nothing on but their lipstick cavorting round
the green – and it's Mummy and I who get blamed.
If you value our friendship – which I do less and less
– kindly stop this ridiculous behaviour at once.

Emily

3rd January

As I write this letter, ten disgusting old men are prancing about all over what used to be the garden – before the geese and the swans and the cows got at it; and several of them, I notice, are taking inexcusable liberties with the milkmaids. Meanwhile the neighbours are trying to have us evicted. I shall never speak to you again.

Emily

This is the last straw. You know I detest bagpipes.
The place has now become something between
a menagerie and a madhouse and a man from the
Council has just declared it unfit for habitation.
At least Mummy has been spared this last outrage;
they took her away this afternoon in an ambulance.
I hope you're satisfied.

5th January

Sir,

Our Client, Miss Emily Wilbraham, instructs me to inform you that with the arrival on her premises at half-past seven this morning of the entire percussion section of the Royal Liverpool Philharmonic Orchestra and several of their friends she has no course left open to her but to seek an injunction to prevent your importuning her further.

I am, sir, Yours faithfully,

G. CREEP,
Solicitor at Law